Click It

COMPUTER FUN

Social Studies

By Lisa Trumbauer

M

The Millbrook Press
Brookfield, Connecticut

Produced by 17th Street Productions, Inc.
33 West 17th Street
New York, NY 10011

Editor, Liesa Abrams
Cover illustration by Sam Ward
Interior design and illustrations by Sydney Wright

Library of Congress Cataloging-in-Publication Data

Trumbauer, Lisa, 1963-
      Click it! Computer fun social studies / by Lisa Trumbauer.
            p.   cm.
      Summary: Explains how to use a personal computer to complete activities related to social studies, such as drawing maps, putting out a community newsletter, and creating a local time line.
      ISBN 0-7613-1656-6 (lib bdg) — ISBN 0-7613-1290-0 (pbk)
      1. Social sciences—Computer-assisted instruction—Juvenile literature. 2. Social sciences—Study and teaching (Primary)—Juvenile literature. [1. Social sciences. 2. Computers.] I. Title: Computer fun social studies. II. Title.
LB1530.T78   2000
372.83'044—dc21   99-052759

1 3 5 7 9 10 8 6 4 2

CONTENTS

Introduction 4

CHAPTER ONE: Cool Communities
Welcome! 9
Main Street 11
Working Wonders 13
Hot Topics 15

CHAPTER TWO: The Bigger Picture
Map It Out 17
Sensational Symbols 19

CHAPTER THREE: Across the Country
Climate Control 22
Clued In 26

CHAPTER FOUR: Around the World
Fabulous Foods 28
Celebrate This! 31

Now What?!

Are you ready to find out all the things you can do on and with your computer? Are you interested in exploring the topic of social studies? You can do both at the same time with the activities in this book!

Why Social Studies?

Social studies touches on many aspects of the world around you. You can learn about people and places from the past, and also about current events. In this book you'll start with your neighborhood, learning more about the community you live in. Who are the people who live and work there? Then you'll see what's interesting about a larger community, your state or province. What's the weather like? What's the motto? Next you'll look at your whole country, and finally the entire world!

But since this is a *computer* book, you have to know some of the basics first. Here's your computer, inside and out:

What it is: You know that big screen that looks like a TV? That's the **monitor**.
What it does: It shows you what you're working on.

What it is: See all the buttons with letters and numbers on them? They're on the **keyboard**.

What it does: Here's where you type in what you want the computer to do and also all the words you want to appear on the screen.

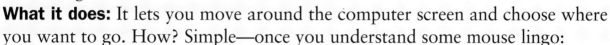

What it is: Can you find the funky-looking curvy tool with one or two big buttons on it? That's the **mouse**.

What it does: It lets you move around the computer screen and choose where you want to go. How? Simple—once you understand some mouse lingo:

Cursor: This shows you where you are on the computer screen. Depending on which program you're in, it may look like a blinking line, an arrow, or an icon. In the **Paint** program, you can move the cursor by moving the mouse.

Click: When the instructions tell you to "click," you push the left button on the mouse and then release it quickly.

Drag: When you need to "drag" the cursor across the screen, you hold down the left button on the mouse and move it across the **mouse pad** it's resting on.

Write On

For the activities in this book, you'll need to understand how to use the **word-processing** program. That's what you use for writing, like when you want to write notes to a friend or make up a story about all your wild adventures as captain of a spaceship. Many different **word-processing** programs are available, but one of the most popular is **Microsoft Works**. The following activities are based on this program, but you can do them with any other program that your computer has. Here are some tips on how to use **Microsoft Works**:

Click on the word **Start** at the bottom of your computer screen. See that list of words above it? Move your mouse up until the word **Programs** is highlighted, then move your mouse to the right and you'll see the names of all your computer's programs. Look for **Microsoft Works**. Found it? Great! Click on it once, and then you'll see three choices. Click **Works Tools** once, then **Word Processor** once. Easy enough, right? Now you should have a blank screen, just waiting for you to fill it up with your writing!

At the top of the screen you'll see some words. This is called the **Menu Bar**. Move your mouse to one of these words, and an arrow will appear. Click, and you'll get a list with more words, called **commands**. You use them to tell your computer what to do. Here are the commands you will use:

- In **File:** Save, Page Setup, and Print
- In **Edit:** Cut, Copy, and Paste
- In **Insert:** ClipArt, Drawing, and Object
- In **Format:** Font and Style

Below the **Menu Bar** you will see a row of small pictures. This is the **Tool Bar**. The **Tool Bar** lets you do some things without using a command. For example:

Font Box: This is the first thing you see on the left. It tells you the name of the type style, or font, that you are using. You can choose a new font (**FONT**, font, **font**, *font*) by clicking the arrow to see your choices, then clicking on the one you want.

Numbers: These numbers tell you the size of your type. Click on the arrow to see how large or small you can make the type—small, normal, huge!

B I U: These three boxes let you change the way the type looks.

B stands for boldface. It makes the type **darker**.
I stands for italics. It makes the type *slanted*.
U stands for underline. It draws a line <u>under the type.</u>

Lines: You might see three or four boxes with straight lines in them. These let you move the words you type to different parts of the screen. You can choose to put them all the way to the left, in the middle (centered), all the way to the right, or all lined up on both sides (justified).

Before you begin to type, choose a font and a size. You can do this on the **Tool Bar** by clicking a new font or type size. You can also do this by clicking **Format**, then clicking **Font and Style**. Here you will see fonts and sizes and **colors!** Choose a color, just as you would a font or a size—by clicking the arrow beside the **Color Box** to see the choices, then clicking the color once. When you've made all your choices, click the **OK** button to return to the main screen.

Paint Up a Storm

So now you're an expert at the writing stuff. What else is there? Painting! Did you know you could be a master artist without picking up a single paintbrush? You can actually paint pictures on your computer! Since you'll be doing a lot of that in the activities in this book, here's a guide to your **Paint** program:

Click on the word **Start** at the bottom of your screen. Remember this list? Click on **Programs** again, but this time choose the word **Accessories**. Yes, there's *another* list of choices. See the word **Paint**? You guessed it—that's where you click!

Whoa! Look at all your paint tools! And colors! Here's what some of the tools in the **Tool Box** can do:

- Pencil: draws a line
- Paintbrush: paints a thicker line
- Paint Can: fills an object with color
- Spray-Paint Can: makes splotchy, star bursts of color
- "A" Icon: makes a box for you to type in
- Shapes: these make exact shapes
- Dotted-Line Box: can move or delete art or type
- Eraser: erases color

To change a color, just click the color you want in the **Paint Box**. If you click the **Paint Box** twice, you'll get a grid with even more colors!

HINT!

Okay, we know the pictures you paint will be totally amazing, but just in case you want to sneak in some of the stuff by the pros, here's how to do it: ClipArt. These are pictures that have already been drawn and are stored inside your computer. In your word-processing program click Insert, then ClipArt. You'll see pictures of all kinds of things, from flowers to people to computers! Click the arrows to move the list up and down to see them. (This is called scrolling.) Then click once on the picture you want. A box will appear around it. Click the Insert button. The picture will appear on your word-processing page! The clip art in this book comes from sources other than Microsoft Works, and you can always buy software that contains more clip art!

PSST!

Exit the Paint program by clicking the box with the X in the upper-right corner.

Now that you know how to write and draw on the computer, there are only two more things to learn before you get started on the *fun* part—the activities! What good would your work be if you couldn't show it off to people? How do you do it? Easy—**Save** and **Print**.

Saving

Click on the word **File** at the top of the screen, then click **Save**. A box called **Save As** will appear. This box may have some folders in it. **Folders** are where the documents you save are kept. Choose a folder to keep your work in, or create a new folder. At the top of the **Save As** box, you'll see a folder with a star beside it. Click it once. In the box that appears, type the name you want to use for your folder over the highlighted words **New Folder**. Then hit the **Enter** key twice, which will open up your new folder. Type the name of your document in the white box that says **File Name**. Click the **Save** button. Your work has been saved!

Once you've saved your file, you'll want to print it out (see below) or start a new one. Click into **File**, then **New** to start a new page. Your old art will disappear, and a new, clean canvas will take its place. To open the file again, click **File**, then **Open**. Click on the name of your file once, and click the **Open** button again. Your work will appear!

Now Print!

You'll have to print out your "paintings" to put together mobiles, posters, and other projects. It would be best if you had a color printer. If not, don't worry!

1. Click **File**, then **Print**.

2. A box with print choices will come on the screen. Some of the activities in this book work better if you choose to print your page in the **Landscape** format. When you need to do that, the instructions will explain how. Otherwise just click **OK**, and your page will print.

That Should Do It!

The activities in this book are based on Windows 95, using **Microsoft Works** and the **Paint** program. Many versions of **Microsoft Works** exist, so yours might be a little different, or you may have a different **word-processing** or drawing program. You may have to alter the instructions slightly to fit your computer. Also, the pictures show how a finished product *may* look. Don't worry if your art looks a bit different. It probably will! That's because you used *your* ideas and *your* computer!

Computers can do all sorts of things, and you're about to see that for yourself. Your computer will be a big help as you learn all about social studies. Experiment with the activities by choosing different fonts, sizes, and colors. Be creative, be an explorer, and have a blast!

Chapter One

Cool Communities

Some people live in big cities, some people live in small towns, and other people live on farms. But all of these people live in *communities*. Your community is your neighborhood. A community has homes where people live. It also has businesses like grocery stores, movie theaters, and restaurants. Most important, a community has people in it, like you and your family!

SOCIAL STUDIES Welcome!

Most communities have welcome signs that tell visitors what's special about the place. The signs include information like *population* (how many people live in the town) or when the town was first *established* (that means when the town was founded). Make a welcome sign on your computer to tell everyone what's special about your community.

Steps:

1 First you have to find the facts. You'll need to do some *research*, which means gathering information. There are a few ways to do research. You can go to your local library or local historical society for help, or you can look things up on the Internet on your computer. You can also talk to people who live and work in your community. Ask them what they know about the history of the community.

2 Once you have some interesting information about your town, go into the **Paint** program.

3 First make the outline for your sign. Click on the **Rectangle** tool, then move your cursor to the top-left corner of the canvas on your screen. Hold down the mouse button and drag the mouse to make a rectangle that stretches across the entire canvas. If you're unhappy with your rectangle, click **Edit,** then **Undo.** Your rectangle will disappear. Now make a new rectangle.

4 Once you're happy with the rectangle, start decorating the inside. First use the **Paintbrush** tool to make the word *Welcome* in big letters. Don't forget to make the word *to* and then the name of your community.

5 Experiment with the different **Paint** tools to draw pictures of things in your town. Use the **A icon** to type information. Click on the **A icon,** then move your cursor to the area of the canvas where you want the words to be. Hold down the mouse button and drag the mouse to make a text box. Type your words in the text box.

6 When you're finished with your welcome sign, **Save** it and **Print** it out. First click **File,** then **Page Setup.** See the box with the title **Orientation?** Click the word **Landscape.** Then click **OK.**

7 Glue your sign to poster board to make it sturdier. Hang the welcome sign on your door. **Print** out more copies and hang them around the neighborhood for everyone to see!

Make welcome signs for communities that are even smaller than your neighborhood, like your school or your home.

SOCIAL STUDIES Main Street

Most communities have a "main street," or a center of town. This is usually where the important buildings are, like the town hall and the post office. There are usually stores there too. Create a 3-D model of the center of your community that shows all the buildings important to your town—and to you!

Steps:

1 Go into the **Paint** program. Choose a building, such as the library. Instead of drawing what the library building looks like, you're going to make a picture of things that represent the library. With the **Rectangle** tool, make a big rectangle for the outline of the library picture—remember, the printout will be much smaller than the picture on your screen.

2 Use the **A icon** to write the word *Library* at the top of the rectangle.

3 With the different **Paint** tools, draw pictures of things you find in the library. You can draw books, magazines, computers, or anything else that your local library has. You can even draw a picture of the librarian if you want! Don't forget to use the **Paintbrush** and **Pencil** tools, and the **Paint Can**.

4 When you're happy with the design for the front of the building, **Save** it and **Print** it out.

5 Repeat steps 1 through 4 to make more building pictures. You can make the police station, the firehouse, a bakery, or anything else you can think of. The pictures can be the same size or different sizes. It's up to you!

PSST!

Make sure all the lines of your shapes are closed, like a border. If they're not, the entire screen will fill with color. Don't panic! Click Edit, then Undo. The color will disappear. Use the Magnifier tool to find the place where the lines aren't connected. Then use the Straight-Line tool or the Pencil tool to close up the shape.

6 Once you've made all the building pictures for the center of your community, get some empty single-serving cereal boxes and other boxes. Glue each building picture to the front of a box to make a 3-D building. Then arrange the buildings the way they're arranged in real life. You have a model main street!

7 Show your model town to family and friends.

Working Wonders

The people who work in a community are the *workers*. Workers who make or grow things are *goods workers*. They provide goods for people, like food or clothing. The other type of workers are *service workers*. Service workers provide services to help people in the community. Make a collage (that's a fancy art word for gluing a bunch of pictures together on paper) that shows different kinds of workers.

1 First think about the workers you want to put on your collage. Choose three goods workers and three service workers. Is there a librarian you like at the library? Is there a baker who makes the best cookies ever? Have you ever been sick and gone to the doctor? Remember that goods workers make or produce things that you use, while service workers offer a service.

2 Go into the **Paint** program. With the **Paint** tools, draw your first worker. You can use the **Ellipse** tool to make the worker's head. For the body use the shape tools for exact shapes or use the **Pencil** or **Paintbrush** to draw wavy outlines.

3 Now draw something that shows what your worker does. For instance, if he's a librarian, you can draw a book in his hands. If she's a baker, you can draw a bunch of cookies around her. Once you're finished with your worker picture, type a label beneath it. Click the **A icon** and make a text box below your art. Then type in the name of your worker, like *Police Officer* or *Shoemaker*.

Police Officer

Shoemaker

4 **Save** your worker picture and **Print** it out. Repeat steps 2 and 3 to make pictures of the other workers. Make sure you draw each worker on a new screen so that you can make the pictures big enough. Remember to make three of each kind of worker!

5 Now make the labels for your collage. With the **Paintbrush** tool make the words *Service Workers*. Choose any color but make the words as big as possible on your screen. **Print** out the words. Then make the words *Goods Workers*. (If you like, choose a different color from the one you used for *Service Workers*.) **Print** out the words.

6 Get some poster board. Divide it in half by drawing a line or gluing a strip of construction paper down the center. Glue the words *Goods Workers* at the top of the left section of the poster board. Then glue the words *Service Workers* at the top of the right section of the poster board.

7 Cut out all your worker pictures. Then arrange them on the poster board, keeping the service workers separate from the goods workers. When you're happy with your collage, glue down the art. Hang up your collage for everyone to see!

Local newspapers report the news and current events going on in communities. Here's your chance to be a reporter and make a newsletter for your neighborhood, street, or apartment building!

Steps:

1 First do some reporting! That means you have to explore your neighborhood and find stories to report. You can write about a news event, like a town parade. You can also interview someone who has worked in your neighborhood for many years. Learn what changes he or she has seen in your community over the years. Collect a few different stories for your newsletter.

2 Once you have all your stories ready, type them up. Click **Microsoft Works,** then **TaskWizards,** then **Common Tasks.** You'll see the word **Newsletter.** Click it twice.

3 You might get a message asking you a question. Click "Yes, run the TaskWizards." Then you'll see three choices. Click **One Column,** then click **Create It!** Highlight the word *Newsletter* and type the name of your paper over it. Name your newsletter for your neighborhood.

4 Now type in your name as reporter, since that's what you are! Type it over the words or numbers in the box below the name of the newsletter.

5 Now think of a headline for your first story. The headline is a title for the story, and it's also a short description of what the story is about; for example, "Kitten Gets Stuck in Tree" or "Baker Says Middletown Is Full of History." A headline doesn't have to be a complete sentence. Type the headline over the words in the next box below where you typed your name. Make sure you type each story separately, with its own headline.

6 Add pictures to your stories too. Click **Insert,** then **ClipArt.** Scroll down the pictures until you find one you like. Then click the box that says **Insert.** Once the art is on your newsletter, click on the art so that a box forms around it. See the dots on the box? Move the cursor over a dot on one of the corners of the box until you see the word **Resize.** Hold down your mouse button and move the mouse to change the size of the art.

7 You can move the art too. Click **Format,** then **Text Wrap.** You'll see two choices—**Inline** and **Absolute.** Click **Absolute,** then **OK.** Now click on your art, hold down the mouse button, and move the mouse to move your art.

8 When you're happy with your newsletter, **Save** it and **Print** it out. **Print** lots of copies to pass out to people in your neighborhood.

Rutherford Newsletter

by Nicole Greenblatt

Street Fair Comes to Town

Last Sunday there was a street fair in our town. There were various booths filled with clothing, crafts, jewelry, and food. The weather was warm and sunny, and many people came. The cheese fries were very popular, and all the vendors said the day was a great success!

PSST!

If you're using a different word-processing program, then you won't be able to do this activity exactly as described. Explore your word-processing program until you find a similar way to make a newsletter.

Chapter Two

THE BIGGER PICTURE

You've probably spent time in towns near yours. Chances are, these towns look like your own. And the people in the streets look like the people in your streets. You live in the same climate, share the same interests, and are involved in the same kinds of businesses. In fact, you're all a part of the same bigger community, and probably live in the same county, state, or province. Here's a chance to learn all about that bigger "neighborhood" you live in.

SOCIAL STUDIES MAP IT OUT

How much do you know about where you live? What's the *climate* (that means the weather and temperature) like? Do plants grow there that don't grow in other places? Are there any national landmarks that people come to see? Design a postcard you can send to someone who lives far away to teach that person all about where you live.

Steps:

1 First you need to find out what your state or province looks like. Look at a map or an atlas or even a travel guide for your area. Or check it out on the Internet!

2 Once you have a picture of the shape of your state or province, go into the **Paint** program.

3 Click on the **Pencil** tool and begin to draw the shape. Make it as big as possible on your screen. (Don't worry if you make a mistake. Click the **Eraser** tool, then erase the part of your shape that you don't like.)

PSST!

Sometimes it can be pretty hard to draw each picture in the right spot. But you don't have to! Draw the picture on an empty part of your screen. Then you can move the picture where you want it. Click the Dotted-Line Box tool on the Tool Bar. Place the cursor above and to the left of the picture you drew, then hold down the mouse button and drag the mouse over the picture. The picture will be inside a dotted-line box. Now move the cursor over the picture until you see a large, dark plus sign. Hold down the mouse button and move the mouse. Your drawing moves! Put your drawing where you want it inside the map.

 4 When you're happy with the shape of your state or province, you can start drawing things *inside* it. Think about what makes your state or province a great place to live in. Here are some ideas of what to draw:

• Draw a star with the **Pencil** or **Paintbrush** in the area where the capital of your state or province is. Use the **A icon** to make a text box below the star. Type the name of the capital.

• Show the climate of your state or province. Is it usually hot and sunny there? If so, draw a big yellow sun on the map. If it rains a lot, draw some raindrops.

• Does your state or province have any big mountains, rivers, or lakes? Draw them too!

• Don't forget to draw a mark for the place where *you* live. With the **A icon**, type the name of your town or neighborhood.

• Are there any special places that visitors like to go to? Any natural parks, amusement parks, or historic sites? Draw *symbols* for these. For example, draw a small tree for a forest, then type the name of the forest below the tree with the **A icon**.

 5 When you're finished, **Save** your map and **Print** it out.

6 Get some construction paper, and cut out a medium-sized rectangle about the size of a postcard. Glue the map to the rectangle. Write the name of your state or province on the construction paper. Then glue the construction paper to poster board to make your postcard sturdier.

7 Finally, glue some blank paper to the other side of the poster board.

8 You'll want to set up the paper like a postcard. Write a few sentences about your state or province on the left side of the blank paper. Explain why you think someone should come visit. Get the name and address of a friend you know in another state or province. Write the person's name and address on the right side.

9 Now attach a stamp to the corner of the postcard, and put the postcard in the mail!

 **SOCIAL STUDIES** SENSATIONAL SYMBOLS

States and provinces use flowers, birds, flags, and other symbols to represent them. Do some research about the symbols of the place where you live, and then put them together for a mobile!

Steps:

1 First you have to find out what the symbols are. You can check out books and read articles in encyclopedias at the library, look up the information on the Internet, or talk to people in your area. If you have a local historical society, look there too. Make a list of all the symbols you learn about. You can use any of the symbols that you think are interesting, but don't forget the flag—that's the most important one!

2 Now go into the **Paint** program. With the **Paint** tools, draw the first symbol on your list. Make it as big as possible on your screen since the printout will be smaller. **Save** the symbol and **Print** it out.

3 Make the rest of the symbols on your list. Make each one on a new screen so that you can make them all as big as possible. **Save** and **Print** each symbol.

4 Get some poster board. Glue your symbols to the poster board to make them sturdier.

5 Now get a hanger and some string. Poke holes in the symbols. Then loop a thread or string through the holes. Finally, tie the thread or string around the hanger to make the mobile.

6 People who see your mobile might want to know where all those symbols come from. When you did your research, did you find out why your state or province uses these symbols and why they are important? Go into your **word-processing** program to make a poster that explains your mobile.

7 Type in the name of the first symbol. You can play with the type if you want. Choose any color, size, or font by clicking **Format,** then **Font and Style.** Below the name of the symbol, give some facts about the symbol. When did it become a symbol for your state or province? Why is it a symbol? If you're describing the flag, what do the colors or pictures on the flag stand for?

8 Hit the **Enter** key several times, then type the name of the next symbol. Now type the information about that symbol. Keep doing this for all of the symbols. You can also type the motto and nickname for your state or province. If you run out of space on the page, start typing on a new page. When you're finished, **Save** and **Print** the pages. Then glue them together on the wall next to your mobile.

Choose another state or province that's nearby or where a friend lives, and make a symbol mobile for that place too! You'll learn interesting facts about other places by seeing what their symbols are and why they're different from yours.

White Oak Tree

The white oak tree was designated the Maryland state tree in 1941. The tree is found commonly throughout the state.

THE FLAG

The Maryland state flag has two designs on it: a black-and-gold design and a red-and-white design. The black-and-gold design is from the Calvert family crest, since Maryland was founded as an English colony by Cecil Calvert in 1634. The red-and-white design is from the Crossland family.

The Black-Eyed Susan

The black-eyed Susan has been the Maryland state flower since 1918. It was chosen because its colors match the Calvert shield, and because it is commonly found in fields and by roadsides.

The Baltimore Oriole

The Baltimore oriole was named the state bird in 1947. It has the same colors as the Calvert shield.

Chapter Three

ACROSS THE COUNTRY

Your country has a lot to do with who you are. All the people who live in one country share certain things in common. They must obey certain laws, and they usually speak the same language. They watch the same television programs at home and see the same movies in movie theaters. In this chapter you can explore your country—on the computer!

 **SOCIAL STUDIES** ## CLIMATE CONTROL

Even though people who live in the same country have so much in common, two areas in a country can still seem completely different. For instance, the weather can be different. The weather affects the clothes people wear, the types of homes they live in, the crops farmers grow, and even the games people play!

Steps:

1 Find a copy of your local newspaper, and look for the national weather map. Check the index to see where the weather map is located. What kinds of weather do you see? Is there a wide variety? Is it wet and rainy in one area and sunny in another? Is the temperature very different on one side of the country from what it is on the other side?

2 Go into the **Paint** program. Click on the **Pencil** tool, and try to draw an outline of your country. Make the outline as big as possible on your screen. If you make a mistake, just use the **Eraser** tool to erase any lines that you're not happy with.

3 **Save** your country map and **Print** out seven copies. Label each one for a different day of the week, from Monday through Sunday.

4 Now look at the symbols that your newspaper used on the weather map to show different kinds of weather. Think of some symbols for the weather map you're making. Think about symbols that show what people need when they're in different kinds of weather. Here are some ideas:
- An umbrella for rain
- A pair of sunglasses for sunshine
- Shorts or a T-shirt for a very hot day
- Mittens or a scarf for a very cold day
- A sled for snow

5 Make the symbols on your computer, using the different **Paint** tools. You can make several symbols on one screen, as long as they fit. You can also make the symbols on new screens if you need more room. **Save** your weather symbols and **Print** them out. **Print** out several copies of all the symbols. Cut out the symbols.

6 Start on a Monday, and check the weather map in your newspaper to see what the predicted weather for that day is across the country. Then glue the weather symbols you made onto your Monday map. Do this every day of the week so that all seven of your weather maps show what the weather was predicted to be across the country for that week. Do you see any patterns? Are some areas always colder or hotter? Does it rain or snow more in some areas?

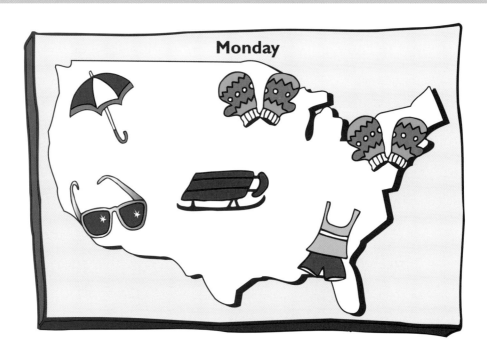

7 Get some poster board. Glue all seven of your maps on the poster board. Look at your weather poster, and think about what those different climates mean for the people who live in them. What is the climate like where you live? Are there things that you enjoy doing that would be hard to do if the weather were different?

8 Go into your **word-processing** program. Click **Insert,** then **Table.** Scroll down the list of tables, and choose any kind of table you want. You might end up with a table that looks like the one on the next page. Any table you make will work fine, though. Choose two columns and as many rows as you like. Then click **OK.**

9 Click **View,** then **Gridlines.**

10 Type the name of your state or province in the top row of the first column. Then hit the **Tab** key. Now your cursor should be in the top row of the second column. Check your weather map poster to find a place where the weather predictions were very different from the place where you live. Type the name of that place in the top row of the second column.

PSST!

If you don't have Microsoft Works, then you can't do this activity exactly as described. Explore your word-processing program to find another way to make a similar table.

11 Hit the **Tab** key again, and now type something that you can do where you live because of the weather. In the other column type something that you would be able to do if you lived in that place.

12 Now type other differences between the two areas in the remaining columns of your table. Think about the type of clothes people would wear, and the different activities that would be possible. You can do some research or ask people you know for ideas.

13 **Save** and **Print** your table. Now glue the table onto the poster board with your weather poster. Hang it up on your wall for everyone to see!

Colorado	Florida
You can snowboard	You can water-ski
You can go mountain climbing	You can go scuba diving
You wear warm clothes, like coats, mittens, and snow boots	You wear T-shirts, shorts, and bathing suits

Every country has *landmarks,* which are famous features (natural or man-made) that people are familiar with. For example, the Statue of Liberty is a landmark in the United States. And the CN Tower is a landmark in Canada. Landmarks can be buildings (like the Empire State Building), monuments (like the Washington Monument), mountains (like Mount Everest), waterfalls (like Victoria Falls), or anything that represents a country. Here's how to make a fun mystery card about the landmarks in *your* country!

Steps:

1 Think about the landmarks in your country. You probably know some of them already. Look in travel guides and geography books at the library for more ideas. Choose landmarks that won't be too hard to draw.

2 Go into the **Paint** program. First make the front of the card—the clue part! Draw one part of the landmark that most people would be able to recognize. For instance, if the landmark you're thinking about is the Statue of Liberty, you could draw the torch she holds in her hand. Make the picture as big as possible on your screen.

3 Click on the **A icon** and make a text box. Inside the box type the questions *What am I?* and *Where am I?*

4 Save the page and **Print** it out.

5 Now you're going to make the inside of your card, with the answer to the mystery—the whole landmark.

COOL iDEA!

You could also come up with a rhyming riddle to help your friends figure out the landmark. For instance, for the Statue of Liberty you could type: *I welcome all to this land, and I hold this torch in my hand.* Type your riddle in the text box you made.

26

6 On a new screen use the **Paint** tools to make the entire landmark. **Save** your landmark and **Print** it out.

7 Go into the **word-processing** program. Type in the name of the landmark and where it's located. You can also type other facts you know about the landmark, such as when it was built, how big it is, or why it's special. **Save** and **Print** the information.

8 Now get a sheet of construction paper. Fold it in half, like a card. Glue the clue you made to the front of the card. Then glue the entire landmark and the information to the inside of the card. Show your card to friends and family, and see if they can guess what the landmark is before they look inside!

What am I? Where am I?

The Statue of Liberty is located on Liberty Island in New York.
It rises more than three hundred feet above the sea. It was given to America by France on the one-hundredth anniversary of U.S. independence.

Chapter Four

Around the World

Do you ever wonder what the world is like beyond your town and even your country? In this chapter you'll learn about the tastes and celebrations of people all over the world!

SOCIAL STUDIES   Fabulous Foods

Some of the foods you eat might come from the country that you live in. But many are probably from other places. Find out where the foods *you* like come from and make a menu book of favorite foods. Then prepare a special recipe to make one of the dishes yourself!

Steps:

1 Go into the **Paint** program. With the **Paint** tools draw a picture of one of your favorite foods.

2 Click on the **Dotted-Line Box** tool. Move the cursor above and to the left of your art. Hold down the mouse button and drag the mouse to form a dotted box around the art. Now click **Edit**, then **Copy**. **Exit** the **Paint** program.

3 Go into the **word-processing** program. Click **Edit**, then **Paste**. Your art should appear.

4 You can change the size of the art if you want. You can also move the art. See steps 6 and 7 on page 16 for help.

5 Now find out where the food is from! Look in an encyclopedia, or check the Internet. Remember to use the original name of the food, not its nickname. For instance, a hot dog is really called a *frankfurter*. Once you've read a little about the history of the food, type the information next to the art on your word-processing page. Don't forget to type the name of the food at the top of the page! Then **Save** and **Print** the page.

6 Repeat steps 1 through 5 to make pages for all of your favorite foods. Do many of your foods come from the same country? If so, maybe you should travel there someday!

7 Once you've made all the pages, attach them to make a menu book of food facts. Staple them together along the left side so that you can flip through the pages. You can make a cover if you like too. Draw some art in the **Paint** program, then **Copy** and **Paste** the art onto a word-processing page. Type a title for your book, then **Save** and **Print** the cover page. Staple it to the front of your book.

8 Choose one of the foods from your book that is *not* originally from your country. Find a recipe for this food in a cookbook or on the Internet. Make sure it's a simple dish to prepare.

9 Go into **Microsoft Works.** Click **TaskWizards.** Scroll down the list to find the words **User Defined Templates.** Click on those words, and you'll see a new list. Scroll down this list to find **Recipe, full page.** Click on the words twice.

10 First type the name of the dish where it says *Recipe name.* Type your name after the words *From the kitchen of.* Then type how long it takes to make the dish after the words *Preparation time.* Finally, type the number of people who will be able to eat the dish after the words *Number of servings.*

11 Move the cursor under the word *Ingredients.* Hold down the mouse button and drag the mouse over the words on the screen to highlight them. Then hit the **Delete** key to erase the words. Type in the ingredients for your dish.

12 Move the cursor under the word *Instructions.* Delete the words here as you did in step 11. Then type in the directions for making your dish.

13 Save and **Print** your recipe. Then get some help from your parents and cook the dish together!

PSST!

If you don't have Microsoft Works, you can't do this activity exactly as described. Explore your word-processing program to find a similar way to make a recipe.

Spaghetti Marinara

From the kitchen of: Chris Grassi
Preparation time: 30 minutes
Number of servings: 4

Ingredients:

16 ounces spaghetti	2 tbsp. olive oil
1 tbsp. garlic powder	1 16-oz. can tomatoes
1 6-oz. can tomato paste	1 tbsp. sugar
$1\frac{1}{4}$ tsp. salt	

Instructions:

1. In a saucepan, heat garlic powder and olive oil over medium heat for a minute or two, stirring constantly.

2. Stir in tomatoes and remaining ingredients, except for the spaghetti. Cook 20 minutes until thickened, stirring occasionally.

3. In a separate pot, bring water to a boil. Add spaghetti, and cook for 11–13 minutes, stirring occasionally.

4. Serve spaghetti covered in sauce.

Holidays are so much fun—you get to decorate, eat special foods, and sometimes you even get presents. Do any of your friends celebrate holidays that your family doesn't celebrate? Learn about some new holidays, and make cards to give to your friends!

Steps:

1 Think about a holiday, like New Year's. Many people celebrate this holiday on the night of December 31. Do you? Jews celebrate the religious new year in the fall, on a day called Rosh Hashanah. Chinese people have a fifteen-day celebration for the new year. That's a lot of parties! Choose a culture or religion that's different from yours, and find out how those people celebrate New Year's. How did the holiday begin? What kinds of decorations do they use? Are there special foods or colors for the holiday? Research the holiday in encyclopedias, at the library, or on the Internet.

2 Go into the **Paint** program and paint some art for your card. Draw things that are used in the celebration of the holiday. For instance, the Chinese make paper lanterns to decorate their new year's parties. If you chose Chinese New Year, draw some lanterns. You could also draw a food or drink that people have on the holiday. Remember to use all the **Paint** tools to add details to your art!

3 **Copy** your art, then **Exit** the **Paint** program. You can only **Copy** and **Paste** one picture at a time, so if you want to use more than one picture, you'll have to do each one separately.

4 To make the front of your card, go into the **word-processing** program. **Paste** your art onto the page and click it once so a frame appears around it. You can change the size of your art, and you can move it too. See steps 6 and 7 on page 16 for help.

5 Once you have all of your art copied onto the page, type a holiday greeting.

6 You can type *Happy New Year* if you chose the Chinese New Year. Or you can type *Happy Rosh Hashanah* if you chose the Jewish New Year. Don't forget to make your greeting big and use different colors if you like. **Save** the front of your card and **Print** it out.

7 On a new page make the inside of the card. Type the information that you learned about your holiday. **Save** your information and **Print** it out.

8 Now get a piece of construction paper. Fold the paper in half, like a card. On the front of your card glue your greeting with the computer art you made. Inside the card glue your information about the holiday. Then you can write a personal note to your friend. Give the card to someone you know who celebrates the holiday. Or you can give it to someone who *doesn't* celebrate the holiday. That way you'll teach someone else about a new holiday!

9 Repeat steps 1 through 8 to make more holiday cards. Learn about all different kinds of holidays for different religions and cultures. Here are some ideas for holidays you can make cards for: Ramadan (Muslim); Saint Patrick's Day (Irish); Boxing Day (English); July 4 (American); Bastille Day (French); Cinco de Mayo (Mexican); Canada Day (Canadian)